MW00973497

See Sport Run™
Spectator's Guide to Baseball
USA Pro Edition

By
The Minkster™

Published by
Sports Education Enterprises, Inc.

See Sport Run Baseball Spectator's Guide, USA Pro Edition
by The Minkster™

Published by
Sports Education Enterprises, Inc.
191 University Boulevard, #503
Denver, CO 80206
www.SeeSportRun.com

Copyright © 2003 by Sports Education Enterprises, Inc.
All rights reserved. No part of this book, including interior design,
cover design, and icons may be reproduced or transmitted in any
form, by any means (electronic, photocopying, recording, or
otherwise) without the prior written permission of the publisher.

Illustrations by Isaac Hartsell, isaacdesigner@aol.com

Book Design by Nick Zelinger, NZ Graphics, znick4@qwest.net

Manufactured in the United States of America

Library of Congress Control Number: 2003105960

ISBN: 1-932491-00-7

For information regarding bulk purchases
or fund-raising efforts, please contact
Sports Education Enterprises, Inc.
at 1-877-SEE S RUN or sales@SeeSportRun.com.

Limit of Liability/Disclaimer of Warranty:

The publisher and authors have used their best efforts in preparing this guide. The publisher and authors make no representations or warranties with respect to the accuracy or completeness of the contents of this book and specifically disclaim any implied warranties of merchantability or fitness for a particular purpose. There are no warranties that extend beyond the descriptions contained in this paragraph. No warranty may be created or extended by sales representatives or written sales materials. Neither the publisher nor author shall be liable for any loss of profit or any other commercial damages, including but not limited to special, incidental, consequential, or other damages.

See Sport Run™ and The Minkster™ are trademarks of Sports Education Enterprises, Inc.

See Sport Run Spokesanimal

Sherwood O. Forrest, or "Sport" as all his friends call him, is the official spokesanimal for See Sport Run. He brings to you a vast knowledge and love of sports. Having participated in many levels of competition, Sport has decided to use his experiences to help educate people who want to learn more about the games we watch and play.

Sport's Bio

◆ BS in Sports Management from Acorn University (AU).
◆ Three-year letterman in baseball and football at AU.
◆ Played 5 years of professional baseball for the San Francisco Redwoods.
◆ Assistant baseball coach at AU for 5 years following pro baseball career.
◆ Wrote sports column for local paper, *Oak Leaf Post*.
◆ Supports local charity– the Lost Acorn Fund.

Sport enjoys all types of athletic activities and is always getting involved in events. Go to our web site and find out his latest adventure at www.SeeSportRun.com.

TABLE OF CONTENTS

Introduction

This Guide is designed to fill in the blanks in your knowledge about Major League Baseball (MLB), complete with terms, basics of the game, and armchair strategies. You can easily stash this compact booklet in a backpack, diaper bag, fanny pack, or purse when you go to a game. Or keep it close to your comfy chair for when you're watching this all-American sport on TV.

This guide is divided into the following sections for quick reference:

Section 1: What Is All That Stuff Doing on Such a Pretty Lawn?

A baseball field is fairly simple to figure out. From the vantage of ballpark seats or on TV, it's easy to see how the infield, outfield, foul lines, and outfield fence fit together. So this section answers questions like:

- Do you know what the distance is between each base?
- Do you know how to find out the number of runs each team scored in the fifth inning of a game?
- If you are visiting Kansas City, do you know what professional baseball team plays there and in what ballpark?

You'll learn about MLB teams and details about the field. Also, you'll find descriptions of the different scoreboards and how to read box scores.

Section 2: Who Is Running the Show?

Anyone who has seen a baseball game for the first time has figured out that the players are the guys wearing the same outfits. What might not have been obvious were the positions they played and the different roles of each. This section not only covers the players' roles, but also looks at how the coaches and umpires fit into the whole picture. Here you'll find the officiating signals and rules that you'd most likely see during a game.

Section 3: What Is That Called?

Have you ever watched or played the television game show JEOPARDY!? In this game, an answer is presented to contestants who have to come up with the correct question. That's how this section works. If you see something happen during a game and want to know the baseball term to describe it, you'll find it here. Information is divided into these three areas: batting, pitching, and defensive action.

Section 4: What Was He Thinking?

Imagine that you are sitting at a ball game; the home team has two guys on base and only one out. The batter hits a long, high ball close to the outfield fence. The outfielder catches it, but the home crowd cheers. Do you know why? (Hint: find Offensive Moves, Base Running, #5.) This section explains common situations a spectator might see during a game.

Section 5: Water Cooler Stats

In baseball, "ERA" is not the Equal Rights Amendment and "INN" is not a cozy place to stay on vacation. To find out what these and other MLB statistical notations mean, review this section. There are three different areas where statistics are kept:

- Hitting and Fielding Stats
- Pitching Stats
- Team Stats

The sport of baseball is loaded with initials that really do mean something!

Section 6: Baseball Lingo

Many TV and radio networks hire ex-baseball players and coaches to be commentators for games. They often use lingo unique to baseball, and even unique to Major League Baseball. So if any terms that are highlighted in bold throughout this Guide are unclear or unknown to you, this mini-dictionary section easily defines them.

Section 7: Now That You're Hooked

To find out where to get more information beyond this Guide, check out this section.

Are you ready to join baseball fans yelling at the TV and second-guessing calls while standing around the water cooler? Then step up to the plate!

What Is All That Stuff Doing on Such a Pretty Lawn?

Okay, you know baseball is about a bunch of guys throwing a little white ball around a well-manicured lawn, while another guy tries to hit it with a stick. But what else do you know other than some leather (for balls and gloves) and wood (for bats) were transformed to make their play toys?

This section addresses the basics of baseball, introducing you to the teams, venues, field layout, and scoreboards.

Where to Watch Who Play

Have you ever wondered what people are talking about when they say, "the Orioles beat up the Blue Jays" or "the Cubs took on the Diamondbacks?" No, it's not the animal-channel host talking about adventures in the wilderness. It's Major League Baseball (MLB) teams engaging in on-field contests.

Major League Baseball is made up of 30 teams playing in 26 cities in the United States and Canada, in stadium buildings traditionally called *ballparks*. Some are open air, others are domed enclosures, still others have retractable roofs that can be opened or closed depending on the weather. MLB has two leagues with three divisions each.

Listed below are the cities, their nicknames,
and the ballparks where the teams play.

National League (NL)

Divisions	Nicknames	Venues
East		
Atlanta	Braves	Turner Field
Florida (Miami)	Marlins	Pro Player Stadium
Montreal	Expos	Olympic Stadium*
New York	Mets	Shea Stadium
Philadelphia	Phillies	Veterans Stadium (moves into Citizens Bank Park in 2004)
Central		
Chicago	Cubs	Wrigley Field
Cincinnati	Reds	Great American Ballpark
Houston	Astros	Minute Maid Park*
Milwaukee	Brewers	Miller Park*
Pittsburgh	Pirates	PNC Park
St. Louis	Cardinals	Busch Stadium
West		
Arizona (Phoenix)	Diamondbacks	Bank One Ballpark*
Colorado (Denver)	Rockies	Coors Field
Los Angeles	Dodgers	Dodger Stadium
San Diego	Padres	Qualcomm Stadium (moves into PETCO Park in 2004)
San Francisco	Giants	Pacific Bell Park

* Retractable Roof

American League (AL)

Divisions	Nicknames	Venues
East		
Baltimore	Orioles	Oriole Park at Camden Yards
Boston	Red Sox	Fenway Park
New York	Yankees	Yankee Stadium
Tampa Bay	Devil Rays	Tropicana Field**
Toronto	Blue Jays	SkyDome*
Central		
Chicago	White Sox	U.S. Cellular Field
Cleveland	Indians	Jacobs Field
Detroit	Tigers	Comerica Park
Kansas City (MO)	Royals	Kauffman Stadium
Minnesota (Minneapolis)	Twins	Hubert H. Humphrey Metrodome**
West		
Anaheim	Angels	Edison International Field of Anaheim
Oakland	Athletics	Network Associates Coliseum
Seattle	Mariners	SAFECO Field*
Texas (Dallas)	Rangers	The Ballpark in Arlington

* Retractable Roof
** Enclosed Dome

At the end of each baseball season (each team plays 162 games, 81 at home and the remainder on the road), the team with the best record in each of the six divisions is awarded a playoff spot. One additional team from each league gets a "wildcard birth" into the playoffs. (Choosing the wildcard teams can get a bit complicated, but basically it's the team with the best record out of the three second-place finishers in each league.) MLB pairs up the teams, and determines locations and dates for each game of the playoffs.

The first team to win three games (commonly referred to as "winning the best of five") in the first playoff series goes to the next round. These teams are paired for the second round of playoffs; with the winners crowned champions of their respective leagues. The first team to win four games wins the league title and goes on to the World Series.

The **World Series** pits the winner of the National League (NL) championship game against the winner of the American League (AL) championship game. The first team to win four games in this series is crowned the year's world champion.

Sport's Shorts

The oldest league is the NL, which began playing in 1876. The AL joined the organized ranks in 1900. The oldest park still in use is Bean Town's Fenway Park, which opened April 20, 1912. Chicago's Wrigley Field (opened in 1914) is a close second. Cincinnati boasts the newest facility and opened at the start of the 2003 season.

This chart shows how the playoffs are structured.

The regular season usually ends in September (unless there is a strike or other unusual event), with the playoffs following right on its heels. The World Series is typically played in October each year, giving rise to its nickname: "Fall Classic." The winners in 2002 were the Anaheim Angels, who won their first world championship in the history of the franchise (42 years).

I Wouldn't Want to Mow That Lawn

The playing field is divided into two areas: **infield** and **outfield**. The *infield* is the dirt and turf area where the **bases** are located; it's commonly called a *diamond*. Why that name? Because the four bases are positioned exactly 90 feet apart, so it forms a diamond shape when an invisible line connects them all.

The Infield Diamond

Home plate is the base where most of the action takes place, because that's where runs are scored. The team scoring the most runs wins the game. **Batters** (or hitters), the **catcher**, and the **umpire** position themselves at home plate. This is the only base on which a runner can score.

Players (or base runners) run around the bases (commonly referred to as **bags** and **base pads**) in a counterclockwise direction. They have to touch each bag with at least one foot before advancing to the next base. If there is a close play at a base (defenseman, ball, and base runner get there at practically the same time), the runner can touch the bag with any part of his body before being tagged and still be **safe**. The exceptions are:

- *When a batter hits the ball and runs past first base.* In this case, the runner must step on the base but can continue running past it along the foul line without being tagged out. If he misses the base or turns toward second, then he can be tagged out.
- *When a base runner crosses home plate.* In order to score, a player needs to safely touch home plate but can then run or slide past it.
- *Time-out is called on the field.* The umpires are the only participants on the field who can officially stop play. When they do, players are allowed to safely step off base.

To learn more about the strategies of base running and fielding, review the section titled ***"What Was He Thinking?"***

Infield Bases

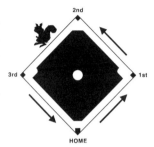

The bases are organized counterclockwise starting with first and ending with home plate, as shown in the diagram. Match the infield location with its name:

    1st = First Base
    2nd = Second Base
    3rd = Third Base
    HOME = Home Plate

The three bases are square in shape and measure 15 inches on each side. They are between three and five inches thick, and filled with varying soft material. Each bag is secured to the ground so it doesn't slide all over the dirt. Having a bag for the infield bases makes it easier for **base runners** to slide into the base and defensemen to feel the base underfoot.

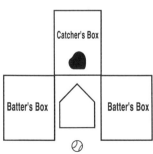

Home plate is in the shape of a square, with the back two corners lopped off. The pointed end, which always points toward the catcher, essentially acts as an arrow showing the pitcher where to throw a strike. Unlike the other bases, home plate is a flat piece of rubber securely fastened in place with a ground anchor.

In addition to the bases around the infield is a **pitcher's mound**. This big mound of dirt in the middle of the diamond has a little white rubber strip on top. It may not look like it, but in all the parks, the pitching rubber is 10 inches higher than home plate. The slope and circumference of the mound can vary from stadium to stadium; however, MLB rules state that the distance from the pitching rubber to the back of home plate must be 60 feet, 6 inches.

Sport's Shorts

In 1969, MLB officials decided that fans wanted more offense in the game. They figured lowering the mound from 15 inches to 10 inches would do the trick, because they expected a lower mound to give hitters a better chance to put the ball into play. They have since figured out there are many influencing factors.

The *outfield* is the wide-open grassy space between the infield and the outfield fence. There is a swath (typically six feet wide) of dirt right in front of the fences encircling the ball field. Called the warning track, it's there to let players know they're close to the fence, stands, **dugout**, or **backstop** when racing to catch a ball popped in the air.

If you have been to different ballparks, you might have noticed that the fences are shaped differently and display different numbers. The numbers correspond to the distance from home plate to that particular location on the field. The minimum distance to the fences for stadiums built after 1958 is 325 feet down the left- and right-field lines, and 400 feet to center field. There are no restrictions on wall height. In older fields (like Fenway Park) fences are higher but distances are shorter, because they had to fit the ballpark into cramped, inner-city blocks.

> ### *Sport's Shorts*
>
> Have you noticed the cool designs in the outfield grass at different ballparks? These decorative designs are the result of a process called *striping*.
> Groundskeepers use rollers to push the grass down, showing the shiny side (dark green) or dull side (light green) to make various patterns.

The last key area of the field to understand is the division between **fair** and **foul** territory. A ball hit *foul* by the batter counts as a strike unless he already has two strikes against him. At that point, he can hit foul balls all day long (as some seemingly do) and not be called out unless a defensive player catches the ball in the air before it touches the ground. A defensive player can get the batter out at any point in the **at-bat** by catching a foul ball (for example, if the hitter has one strike and two balls against him, or even on his first swing of the bat).

To determine if the ball is fair or foul, the umpire looks down the foul line drawn in white chalk from home plate to the **foul pole** in the outfield bleachers. If a fly ball hits first or third base, then bounces into foul territory, it is a fair ball. If a player or umpire touches the ball in fair territory then it is a live ball. If touched and dropped in foul territory then the ball is ruled foul.

The lines and foul poles are considered fair territory so if a player touches a ball while rolling along the white-chalked line, the ball is fair and in play. In the case of a **fly ball**, if it lands outside the white lines, the ball is foul. If it hits the foul pole above the black ring, it's a home run. If the ball hits below the ring and bounces into the field of play, it's a live ball.

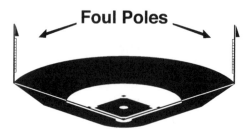

Foul Poles

Although they are not right on the field of play, the **on-deck circle, dugout,** and **bullpen** are important areas around a baseball field. A few feet in front of each dugout, there is a white circle several feet in diameter where the next batter (*on-deck*) gets loose by swinging the bat. Many hitters will watch the pitcher to get a feel for his arm motion and how he releases the baseball. This helps them to get their timing down and recognize pitches when at-bat.

The dugout is the bench area on either side of the infield that looks like a half-buried bus stand. When not involved in active play, the players and coaches are required to stay

> ### Sport's Shorts
> In some parks you will see *fungo circles* somewhere between the **on-deck circle** and the **batter's box**. No, it's not something requiring disinfectant. Coaches use these areas for fielding practice before games. They use a *fungo bat* (longer handle, larger barrel than a regular bat) to hit fly balls to outfielders and ground balls to infielders. This gives them a feel for how the turf and ball will react on that particular day.

in the dugout. In most major league parks the locker rooms are located behind the dugout. If a player or coach gets tossed out of the game, he not only must leave the field, but the dugout as well, and retire to the locker room.

The bullpen is an area around the field (the location varies from ballpark to ballpark) in which the relief pitchers warm up before playing in a game. Some coaches and catchers stay in this area to work with the relief staff.

Bingo Night at the Ballpark

The scoreboard is a spectator's best friend–unless you don't understand how to read it. Some might mistake it for a bingo board! It provides more than the score; it

shows statistics and general information to help fans fol-
low the game. Although scoreboard designs across
Major League ballparks vary, almost all contain these
three distinct areas of interest:

Main Scoreboard

This scoreboard lists the starting players, their jersey
numbers, their defensive positions, and the order they will
bat, from top (who bats first in the game) to bottom. It
shows who is up to bat usually along with that player's hitting stats (see *"Water Cooler Stats"* for translations). The
score by inning is shown along with the total number of
runs, hits, and errors for each team. During each at-bat you
will see the number of balls and strikes against the batter,
and total number of outs in that half of the inning.

A typical MLB scoreboard

Scores Around the League

This scoreboard keeps spectators up to date on games being played that day in MLB. Sometimes there is a section for the National League and one for the American League, with teams listed by cities. This helps the fans distinguish between clubs in the same city (e.g., *NY* Mets in the NL, and *NY* Yankees in the AL) and find specific teams more easily.

The first game in the example below shows that the Colorado Rockies (visiting team) are ahead of the Los Angeles Dodgers (home team) 5 runs to 2 in the top (T) of the 3rd inning (3), with #34 pitching for Colorado and #43 pitching for L.A. The second shows the Cincinnati Reds defeated the Chicago Cubs on a final (F) score of 6 runs to 3, with #36 pitching at the end of the game for the Reds and #44 for the Cubs. This is a typical scoreboard and most stadiums have a similar version.

Pitching Info

This scoreboard shows the type of pitch just thrown, speed of that pitch in miles per hour (MPH), total number of pitches thrown, total balls called, and total strikes called for the pitcher currently on the mound. In the example below, the pitcher just threw a 96-mph **fastball** on his 78th pitch of the game, and has thrown a total of 35 balls and 43 strikes in the game. (You'll notice that if the balls and strikes are added together it totals the number of pitches.)

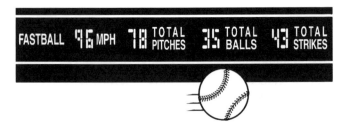

There can also be other scoreboards displaying information unique to a particular stadium. Don't be afraid to ask a fellow fan or usher what a random acronym posted on the scoreboard means. If you leave your seat to get peanuts or a hot dog, now you know what to look for on the scoreboard when you get back.

Even if you don't go to games, you can use this new-found knowledge to catch up on statistics published in newspapers or on the Internet. They feature similar information when reporting the results of games called **box scores**. Using what you have learned in this section, coupled with the *"Water Cooler Stats"* section, you should have no problem reading the box scores of your favorite team.

In addition to the box scores, you'll find standings listed online and in newspapers. This shows where your favorite teams are in the standings, and how many games they are behind the first-place team; or if your team is leading and how far it is ahead of the competition.

CENTRAL	W	L	PCT	GB	HOME	ROAD	EAST	CENT	WEST	NL	L10	STRK
TWINS	53	40	.570	-	31-17	22-23	8-9	21-14	14-9	10-8	6-4	W1
WH SOX	44	49	.473	9.0	26-21	18-28	5-5	21-19	10-15	18-10	3-7	W1
INDIANS	41	49	.456	10.5	23-20	18-29	11-17	19-23	5-7	6-12	4-6	W1
ROYALS	35	54	.393	16.0	21-21	14-33	2-11	19-17	9-13	5-13	4-6	W2
TIGERS	34	56	.378	17.5	20-23	14-33	5-11	19-26	4-7	6-12	7-3	L1

In the example showing the American League Central Division, left to right are:

- Team nickname
- Total number of games won (W)
- Total number of games lost (L)
- Winning percentage (PCT)
- Games behind the leader (GB)
- Home record showing wins first and losses second (HOME)

- Road record listed in the same manner (ROAD)
- Record against teams in the American League East division (EAST)
- Record against Central division (CENT)
- Record against Western division (WEST)
- Record against National League (NL)
- Record over the last ten games played (L10)
- The current streak (STRK) with W# showing how many games won in a row, and L# showing the number lost in a row beginning with the most recent game played and counting backwards.

Especially as it gets close to playoff time, the most important number is the *Games Behind* (GB). It shows division leaders and how close the other teams are to tying for the number one spot. You will also see a list of potential wildcard teams for each league, along with the number of games behind for the wildcard.

Who Is Running the Show?

Three groups make up every MLB game: umpires, coaches, and players. The umpires ensure everyone plays by the rules, and make final calls on close plays throughout the game. Coaches orchestrate the plays and manage the personnel with the intent to win the game. Players are, of course, the athletes in uniform whom we all love to watch.

Umpires and Their Gestures

In no other major professional sport is the officiating crew (umpire staff) key in every play. The home plate umpire calls each pitch a ball or strike. If the ball is hit fair, he determines if the runner is safe or out. (You can pick out the umpires easily; they are wearing the solid black, grey, tan, or traditional blue uniform.) You'll see four umpires on the field in a regular season game; two more are added during playoff games. The additional staff is used to provide better coverage during critical games.

Sport's Shorts

Fans are often second-guessing calls by the umpires, especially if one goes against their favored team. When raucous fans want to make it known that a call is questionable, they sometimes address the umpire as "Blue!" and yell suggestions such as, "Hey, Blue! Get a refund on that LASIK surgery!"

PARTICIPANTS

- *Home Plate Umpire (HPU)*
  Positioned behind the plate, wearing protective gear, including a face mask.
- *First Base Umpire (FBU)*
  Positioned near first base to make line calls and plays at first. Assists with **check swing** calls on batters and other general calls.
- *Second Base Umpire (SBU)*
  Positioned behind second base near the infield/outfield break. Makes calls at second, and assists on general calls.
- *Third Base Umpire (TBU)*
  Positioned near third base to make line calls, and plays at third. Assists with check swing calls on batters and other general calls.
- *Right Field Umpire (RFU)*
  Used only in **postseason games**.
  Assists the first base umpire.
- *Left Field Umpire (LFU)*
  Used only in postseason games. Assists the third base umpire.

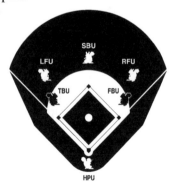

To convey calls effectively to players, coaches, and spectators, the officiating team uses hand signals and verbal expressions. These eight basic signals are important to recognize and know what they mean:

Sport's Shorts

Have trouble keeping straight which is left field and which is right? Imagine yourself in the catcher's position looking at the outfield. On your right is the right field line and right fielder; on your left is the left field line and left fielder.

- **Strike**
  Right hand is usually pumped outward, sometimes pointed to the right with the umpire's head turned in the same direction.

- **Ball**
  No hand motion after the pitch.

- **Out**
  Right hand is curled into a fist, elbow bent, sometimes pumped forward and back, in front of the body.

- **Safe**
  Hands open with the palms down; arms make a sweeping motion from the center of the body, out to the sides, ending with arms pointing out from both sides in a "T" shape.

Strike

Ball

Out

Safe

PARTICIPANTS

PARTICIPANTS

- **Fair**
  Arm straight out, pointing to
  the fair part of the field.

Fair

- **Foul**
  Both arms straight up,
  pointing to the sky.

- **Time**
  Both arms straight up, same as   Foul & Time
  a foul ball. Play is stopped.

- **Count**
  Hands above the head, left hand holding
  up the number of fingers representing
  balls, right fingers show strikes.

Count

In addition to hand and body signals, sometimes the umpire will shout a call–typically with *time*, *safe*, and *out* calls. If you miss seeing and hearing a call, use the scoreboard to figure it out or watch what happens next on the field. If all else fails, ask the person sitting next to you. Baseball fans are usually a friendly lot.

All the Team's Coaches

Baseball is the only major sport in which the head coach is called a **manager**, and all of the coaches wear the team uniform during a game. It's a good thing, because I don't think kicking dirt at an umpire in wing tips, a suit, and tie would be as effective.

There are usually six coaches on a team in addition to the manager.

- *Bench Coach*
  In the **dugout** with the manager during games. Helps with the strategy and general game management.
- *Bullpen Coach*
  In the **bullpen** where the pitchers warm up. Works with the **relievers** during a game.
- *First Base Coach*
  The coach in the coach's box behind first base while the team is on offense. Assists with play calling and base running management.
- *Hitting Coach*
  Works with hitters during batting practice before the game.
- *Pitching Coach*
  In the dugout. Focuses on the pitcher currently playing. Goes out to the mound to talk during a game with pitchers who are struggling.
- *Third Base Coach*
  The coach in the coach's box behind third base while the team is on offense. Assists with play calling and base-running management.

These coaches have additional responsibilities outside of the game environment, and play key roles during a game. The first- and third-base coaches are only on the field when their team is on offense; they signal in plays

PARTICIPANTS

called from the bench to their offensive guys on the field. These signals tell the batter and runner what to do so they both work together to get in a position to score.

The on-field coaches stand in the coach's box behind their respective bases. Sometimes you will see them standing outside the white lines. It isn't a hard-and-fast rule that they stay within the box, but if the opposing team complains to the umpire it will be strictly enforced–on both teams.

The pitching coach sometimes goes to the mound and talks to pitchers during games to calm them down. He also makes suggestions on their pitching form and talks through strategy decisions with the pitcher and catcher.

Sport's Shorts

It is against the rules for coaches to argue balks, strikes, and balls but they sure make up for it in other areas. Occasionally you'll see them engage the umpires in a lively discussion over close plays at a base.

During a single inning, the manager or coaches can only go to the mound one time. If any of them returns to the mound during the same inning, the pitcher must be substituted and leave the game–unless the visit is prompted by an injury to the pitcher. The manager is almost always the one to go out and pull the pitcher. Rarely does the pitching coach do this unless the manager gets tossed from the game.

So when you see the manager heading to the mound, it is most likely time for a pitching change–and a good chance for you to make a trip to the concession stand while the **reliever** throws his eight warm-up pitches.

Players: The Guys in the Uniforms

Major League Baseball rules limit the number of players each team can have on their **roster** during a season. Teams can officially have 40 players on their rosters during **Spring Training**, but have to cut their rosters down to 25 for **Opening Day**. Many of the cut players are sent to their team's **minor leagues** (teams in the A, AA, AAA, and Rookie leagues). Teams can expand their roster back to 40 on September 1 of the same year if they wish.

A *regulation* baseball game is made up of nine innings. Each team takes a turn in the field and at-bat to complete an inning. The home team takes the field first (defensive position); the visitors bat first (offensive position). The visitors' at-bat is the **top of the inning**. After

PARTICIPANTS

PARTICIPANTS

the visiting team makes three outs, the home team comes to bat for the **bottom of the inning**.

Defensive players usually set up in the same general locations on the field, although they may adjust their positions in those areas based on the batter at the plate (discussed further in *"What Was He Thinking?"*). The only equipment they use in the field is a glove. Players' gloves vary in size and shape, depending on the position played (generally larger in the outfield, smaller in the infield) and each player's preference.

Each field position is assigned a number in order to easily track on a scorecard–a shorthand method to keep stats. On a ballpark scoreboard, you'll see an abbreviation used instead of a number to show the position each player is assigned.

Match the position on the field with their scoreboard reference (Letter) and scorecard number (Pos #).

Position	Letter	Pos #
Pitcher	P	1
Catcher	C	2
First Base	1B	3
Second Base	2B	4
Third Base	3B	5
Shortstop	SS	6
Left Field	LF	7
Center Field	CF	8
Right Field	RF	9

PARTICIPANTS

It is important to note: these position numbers are *reference numbers*. The jersey numbers are not related in any way.

You can keep score in baseball by not only recording how many runs are produced in an inning but also by tracking how the different outs and runs are made. You can track information such as **strikeout** ("K"), *base on balls* ("BB"), **line drive** ("L") and **sacrifice fly** ("SF") on a baseball scorecard. These scorecards are usually sold at ballparks, sports stores, and on the Internet.

There are nine starting players (the same ones you see listed in the **batting order**) out of the 25 on the roster for each team. In the American League only, an additional batter (**designated hitter**) is listed on team rosters. This

PARTICIPANTS

Sport's Shorts

Some of the many awards given to top players at the end of a season are:

Cy Young
Gold Glove
MVP
Manager of the Year
Relief Man
Rookie of the Year

Some are awarded to two players–one each in the AL and NL. Others have multiple winners regardless of League.

additional offensive player goes to the plate in place of the pitcher in the batting rotation. The home team rules apply (in AL parks, the designated hitter is used; in NL parks it is not).

At the beginning of a game, each manager gives the plate umpire and opposing manager a list of players, their fielding positions on defense, and the order in which they will bat. Once the first pitch is thrown, the **batting order** cannot be changed. One player may be substituted for another; but once the new player hits, the original player is out of the game. (Once a player leaves the game, he cannot return.) A player may be moved from one fielding position to another without leaving the game.

In addition, if a batter attempts to hit out of turn and the opposing team appeals to the umpire, that batter is out. If the opposing team doesn't catch the change before the batter completes his at-bat, then the batter is considered "legal" and the next batter is the player listed behind him in the batting order. The umpire will not make this call without an appeal, since (according to the MLB rulebook) this rule is meant to keep the benches on their toes.

PARTICIPANTS

Basics of the Lineup

- The lead-off hitter is the first to bat at the start of a game and listed first in the batting order.
- The batting order doesn't restart with each inning, but continues through the lineup.
- Players can move around on defense and play different positions, but the order in which each player bats does not change.
- Lineups vary based on factors such as the ballpark, health of the players, starting opposing pitcher, current batting averages, and the manager's gut feeling.

The equipment used by batters or hitters is more for protection than for offensive improvements. Some hitters wear a batting helmet, arm guards, batting gloves, and shin guards. Some just wear the helmet and gloves. The only protection required by MLB is the batting helmet. In addition, bats are required to be made of wood, no more than 42 inches long, round, and less than 2 3/4 inches in diameter. The batter can select the weight he wants.

Defining the Batting Lineup

PARTICIPANTS

BATTING ORDER		OBJECTIVE
Top of the order	1st	The *lead-off* hitter needs to be fast and able to get on base.
	2nd	The *second spot* needs to have someone who can connect with ball & advance the *lead-off* hitter.
	3rd	The *third spot* should be a power hitter who can score base runners and get on base in the process.
Meat of the order	4th	The *cleanup hitter* needs to be the slugger who can clear the bases with extra base hits or home runs.
	5th	The *fifth spot* needs to be a good hitter so the *cleanup hitter* isn't walked for an easy out.
	6th	The *sixth spot* is similar to a *lead-off* hitter but usually isn't as fast and/or has a lower batting average.
	7th	Can you guess? The *seventh spot* is a similar type of player as the *second spot* but not as good an offensive player.
Bottom of the order	8th	The *eighth spot* is typically a player with one of the lowest batting averages on the team or in a hitting slump.
	9th	The *ninth spot* is typically the pitcher in the National League. In the American League this is usually the player with the lowest batting average.

The Special Bond Between Pitcher and Catcher

The catcher is like the director of a movie. He takes the signals from the coaches, keeps track of the various hitters' tendencies, watches for steals, sends signals to the infield defense, tags out players at home plate, and works with the pitcher to figure out the best defensive strategy for each hitter. The most commonly used method to communicate with his teammates on defense is through *pitching signals.*

The catcher needs to communicate the type of pitch to his team without the offense reading his signs. To accomplish this, when he is in the squatting position, he puts his hands close to his body and between his thighs with his gloved hand resting on or hanging next to a thigh. At this point, the batter should be in a ready batting position and the coaches in their respective boxes, putting them at an angle where they are unable to see the catcher's signal.

It is important to note that standard catcher's signals are commonly used throughout baseball. This is possible because the catcher can easily hide his signals from the opposition's players and managers. It is kept simple since catchers work with multiple pitchers during a season (MLB teams used an average of 21 pitchers during the 2002 season). Following are the commonly used catcher hand gestures, with the specialty unique to each pitcher.

PARTICIPANTS

Fastball Curveball Changeup Specialty

- **Fastball:** One finger pointing to the ground.

- **Curveball:** Two fingers pointing to the ground.

- **Change-up:** Three fingers pointing to the ground or a wiggle of the fingers.

- **Specialty**: Four fingers pointing to the ground. Some typical major league pitches:

    - Fastball cutter
    - Forkball or split-fingered fastball
    - Knuckleball
    - Palmball
    - Screwball
    - Sinker or two-seam fastball
    - Slider

Each team handles pitch calls differently, but usually either the coaches or the catchers make the calls for an entire game. Once the signal is given to the pitcher, he can either agree and send the pitch, or shake off the call (slightly shaking his head "no"); the catcher calls another pitch until both agree.

Sport's Shorts

When runners are on base, the catcher flashes several signs in a row, with only the defense knowing which is the real call. Also, catchers may wrap white tape around the tips of their fingers so the signals can be more visible to the pitcher.

In addition to the finger signals to communicate the direction of a pitch, a catcher might tap the inside of his left or right thigh to show where the pitch should end up. He also might move slightly to one side of the plate or the other to help the pitcher focus.

INSIDE PITCH   **OUTSIDE PITCH**

Catchers have to be familiar with all the pitchers in the starting rotation as well as the **bullpen**. There are usually five pitchers on a team's starting rotation; every sixth game day, the same pitcher starts (pitches from the

PARTICIPANTS

Sport's Shorts

Baseballs are made of horsehide and stitched 108 times with red yarn. This gives the pitchers the ability to put *break* (pitch curves sharply as it gets closer to home plate) on the ball. Regulations require that it weigh 5–5 1/4 ounces and have a circumference of 9–9 1/4 inches. Each home team must supply a minimum of 13 new balls for each game.

first inning until the game is over or a **reliever** is put into the game). This standard five-pitcher lineup has evolved over time, just as the typical number of pitches thrown in a game by the starting pitcher has dwindled to 120. These two guidelines are believed to help "save the arm" of starting pitchers to minimize injury and extend careers.

The catcher wears the most equipment when his team is on defense. His gear protects him from errant pitches and home plate collisions with runners. He uses a large, rounded glove with extra padding to catch pitches that come at him 80 to 100⁺ mph.

Catcher's gear

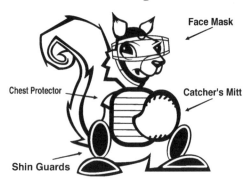

Face Mask

Chest Protector

Catcher's Mitt

Shin Guards

What Is That Called?

If you want to know the word used to describe an action or subject, you may find the lingo difficult to track down. Think about the language pocket-guides that list phrases in English, followed by the specific language translation. They can tell you, for example, how to ask where the train station is in Japanese.

This section takes a similar approach. It addresses game situations from three perspectives: batter, pitcher, and defense. So, if you want to know the term for when a batter has three balls and two strikes against him, look under the *"Batting Terms."* Once you have read a few of them, you'll get the hang of it.

TRANSLATIONS

Batting Terms

What is it when the batter:	Answer:
Can hit successfully from both the right and left side of the plate.	Switch-hitter
Doesn't swing and is called out on a third strike.	Struck-out looking
Doesn't swing at a **pitch** in the **strike zone**, as called by the umpire.	Strike

What is it when the batter:	Answer:
Doesn't swing at a **pitch** outside of the **strike zone** as called by the umpire.	Ball
Has taken more balls than strikes in a single **at-bat** (e.g., three balls and two strikes [3–2], or two balls and no strikes [2–0]).	Ahead in the count
Has taken more strikes than balls in a single **at-bat** (e.g., one ball and two strikes [1–2] or no balls and one strike [0–1]).	Behind in the count
Has three balls and two strikes against him.	Full-count
Hits a ball between two defensive players. For example, a ground ball is hit between the second baseman and third baseman; it goes into the outfield for at least a base hit.	Hit in the gap
Hits a **fly ball** deep into the outfield, it hits the ground and bounces over the outfield fence, the runners are advanced two bases by the umpire.	Ground-rule double

TRANSLATIONS

What is it when the batter:	Answer:
Hits a **fly ball** in fair territory; it doesn't go out of the **infield**. Typically an umpire will yell *infield fly* so all the players know that is the call.	Infield fly and automatic out
Hits a single, double, triple, *and* home run in a single game (in any order).	Hitting for the cycle
Hits the ball and gets on base safely without recording an out.	Successful at-bat
Hits the ball and safely gets on first base with no errors by the defense.	Single
Hits the ball and safely gets on second base with no errors by the defense.	Double
Hits the ball and safely gets on third base with no errors by the defense.	Triple
Hits the ball into the field of play and fair territory, then makes it all the way around the bases to score on that single hit.	In-the-park home run
Hits the ball over the outfield fence in *fair* territory.	Home run

TRANSLATIONS

TRANSLATIONS

What is it when the batter:	Answer:
Hits the ball that allows a runner on base and/or himself to score. For example, there is a runner on base and the batter hits a home run. He would be awarded 2 RBI's.	Runs Batted In or RBI(s)
Hits the winning home run to end a game, which means with one hit the home team's score just jumped ahead of the visitors. It is always a player from the home team who will accomplish this, since they bat last in every inning.	Walk-off home run
Intentionally hits a **fly ball** deep into the outfield, with a runner on base with less than two outs, so the runner advances on the bases.	Sacrifice fly
Stands to the catcher's left in the batter's box.	Right-handed hitter
Stands to the catcher's right in the batter's box.	Left-handed hitter
Steps out of the **batter's box** while the pitcher is in his throwing motion, without getting awarded a time-out from the home plate umpire.	Automatic strike

What is it when the batter:	Answer:
Substitutes for the player who was supposed to bat next in the lineup.	Pinch hitter
Swings and misses on a third strike.	Struck-out swinging
Swings and misses the ball.	Strike
Tries to **bunt** home a base runner on third.	Squeeze play
When a left-handed batter (stands on the right side of home plate) hits the ball into left field, or vice versa.	Hits to the opposite field

TRANSLATIONS

Pitching Terms

What is it when the pitcher:	Answer:
Comes in during a game, completes it, and his team wins.	Save
Has three balls and two strikes on the batter (3–2).	Full Count
Has thrown more balls than strikes to a single batter (e.g., 3–2 or 2–0).	Behind in the count

What is it when the pitcher:	Answer:
Has thrown more strikes than balls to a single batter (e.g., 1–2 or 0–1).	Ahead in the count
Intentionally throws four balls to the catcher (usually standing up and to the side of the hitter and the catcher's box).	Pitchout, intentional walk
Starts his full throwing motion, with his hand in the glove raised at/above his head, accompanied by a high leg kick before delivering the pitch to home plate.	Full windup
Starts his throwing motion toward home plate, but turns and throws to first (assuming there is a runner there), and the umpire tells the **base runner** to go to second.	Balk
Throws a bad pitch that the catcher misses (e.g., up over his head or bounces in the dirt).	Wild pitch or passed ball
Throws for the entire game, and the opposing team doesn't get any hits.	No-hitter

TRANSLATIONS

TRANSLATIONS

What is it when the pitcher:	Answer:
Throws for the entire game, and the opposing team doesn't score any runs.	Shut-out
Throws the ball to the catcher when a batter is in the box.	Delivery or pitch

Defensive Terms

What is it when the defense:	Answer:
Catches the runner (touches the base with the ball in hand) going to the next base on a caught **fly ball** without **tagging-up.**	Doubling up the runner
Gets one runner out, then gets a second out while the same ball is in play.	Double play, or turning a double play
Gets three offensive players out while the same ball is in play.	Triple play or turning a triple play
Has a runner caught between bases, and keeps throwing the ball to teammates until they tag the runner out.	Run down
Has allowed **base runners** to get on first, second, and third.	Bases loaded

What is it when the defense:	Answer:
Misses an easy catch, overthrows a teammate, or makes some other mistake that should have been an out; but the runner ends up safely on base or scoring.	Error
Substitutes two players in the lineup at the same time.	Double switch
Throws a runner out when he is trying to steal a base.	Pickoff

TRANSLATIONS

What Was He Thinking?

On the surface, baseball looks like a simple game. A guy throws a ball, a batter hits it, players in the field try to get the batter out. At the end of the day, each team wants to have more runs than the other to post a win.

But the key to enjoying baseball–more than seeing action on the field–is understanding the *strategy* behind the game. To comprehend the "chess match" within this game, three basic areas of the game must be clear: batter outs, base runner outs, and game-ending scenarios.

Batter Outs

There are many different ways a batter can be called out, some more obscure than others. The most commonly seen ways are:

- Fair or foul fly ball is caught in the air by a fielder.
- Fair ball is hit and batter is tagged before reaching first base.
- Fair ground ball is fielded and thrown to first baseman who tags the bag before the batter can get there.
- Third strike is legally caught by the catcher. If he misses catching the ball then the batter must be tagged out or thrown out at first.
- Bunted ball goes foul on third strike.
- Batter hits an **infield fly** (fair fly ball that doesn't get out of the infield).
- Batter hits a fair ball that touches him before it touches a fielder, while batter is outside the batter box.

STRATEGY

Base-Runner Outs

The best way to think about running the bases is a cat-and-mouse game. The runner tries to get any advantage he can to ultimately score, while the defense tries to get him out before he crosses home plate. Along the way, the runner must avoid certain situations so he isn't called out before scoring as in the following scenarios.

- Runner runs outside the **baseline** to avoid being tagged out.
- Runner intentionally interferes with the fielder's attempt to make a play on a batted or thrown ball.
- Runner gets tagged while off a base (with the exception of running past first after hitting a fair ball).
- Runner gets tagged before returning to the base after a fair or foul fly ball is caught by the defense (**tagging-up**).
- Fielder who has the ball tags the runner or a base (**force play**) before runner gets to a bag. A force play means the runner must advance to the next base, so the defensive player only needs to touch the base to put that runner out.
- Runner who is not standing on base is touched by a fair ball that's just been hit before the ball passes an infielder or is touched by a defensive player.
- Runner passes his own teammate while running the bases before the teammate scores or gets putout.
- Hitter runs past first base then turns to run toward second, but is tagged out before he can get safely to either base.

Game-Ending Scenarios

Baseball offers an endless array of game winning (or losing) stories, but there are some basic rules that create these situations:

- If the home team has scored more runs than the visiting team after the top half of the ninth inning, the game is over (that is, the team doesn't need any more runs to win the game).
- If the visiting team is ahead in runs scored, the home team has a chance to tie or win by scoring one more run than the other team. The game ends once the winning run touches home plate, even if runners are still on base.
- If the game is tied at the end of nine completed innings, the teams play additional full innings until one of the teams scores more runs than the other. (The scenarios listed above hold true for extra innings as well).
- A game can be *called* because of dangerous conditions such as lightning, earthquakes or foul weather conditions.

Remember, the home team always has the last chance to win the game because the home team players bat last in the ninth inning.

Now that you have the basics down, read on for explanations of various situations you'll see on the baseball diamond.

STRATEGY

Offensive Moves

Base Running

Situation #1:

A runner is at first or second. The manager sends in the signal for the runner to steal. (As a spectator, you probably won't know that until the player starts running). The batter is given the signal to swing on the next pitch regardless of whether it's a strike or a ball.

Strategy #1:

This is usually only called by the manager if the batter has fewer than two strikes against him. When the batter swings it gives the runner a chance to successfully steal because, in order to throw the runner out, the catcher has to move his body outside the area where the batter is completing his swing; thus delaying the throw to second or third base. Otherwise, he can throw from his catching position, which gives him a better chance of getting the runner out.

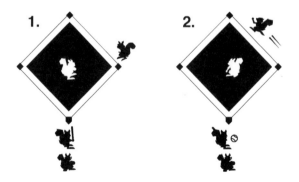

Situation #2:

A base runner gets caught between bases in a run down (see *"What Is That Called"* for definition), but keeps running back and forth between defenders as long as possible.

Strategy #2:

If the player runs outside the **baseline** area, the umpire will call him out without the defense having to tag him. He realizes there's no chance of getting on base safely unless a throwing error occurs. Faced with an inevitable out, the runner continues to run between defensive players, hoping they will make a bad throw so he can proceed safely to base and/or he gives the batter or another base runner enough time to advance an additional base.

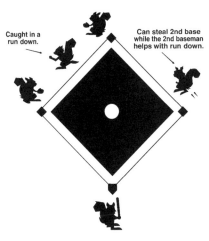

Caught in a run down.

Can steal 2nd base while the 2nd baseman helps with run down.

STRATEGY

Situation #3:

A runner is on third base with no one on second. The hitter just knocked the pitch down into the ground several feet in front of him (a **bunt**).

Strategy #3:

The manager called a **squeeze play**, hoping the runner will beat the throw to home plate. Because the runner can take a lead off the base (he knows the hitter is bunting), there's a good possibility he can get home to score before the defense can make a play on the ball. In a bunt situation, the pitcher, catcher, third baseman, *and* first baseman have to be ready to grab the ball quickly, depending on which direction it goes; one of them has to cover home plate to defend against the squeeze play, or the runner will easily score.

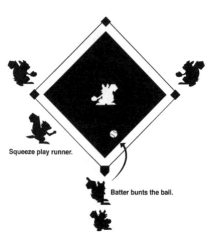

Squeeze play runner.

Batter bunts the ball.

Situation #4:

A runner is on first, and the hitter is ahead in the count. The coach signals for the runner to take off for second (**steal**) while the pitcher is in the process of delivering the throw to home plate (**the stretch**).

Strategy #4:

This offensive play, called a hit-and-run, is used because the manager sees an opportunity to get an extra base hit and score depending on where the ball is hit. When the defensive player sees the runner is going to steal, he has to move over toward second base to make a play. The hitter then tries to hit through the gap created by the defensive adjustment, depending on whether the shortstop or second baseman covers.

The manager typically only calls this when the hitter is ahead in the count (e.g., two balls with no strikes [2–0] or three balls and one strike [3–1]), so the pitcher will be pressed to throw a strike to get an out. Sometimes the defense thinks the hit-and-run has been called, so they **pitchout**, hoping to catch the runner.

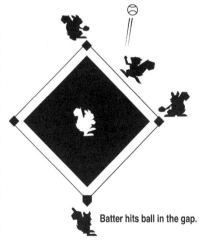

Batter hits ball in the gap.

STRATEGY

Situation #5:

There are runners on first and second with less than two outs in the inning. Each takes several steps toward the next base. The runners position themselves so they can see the pitcher while being able to make a quick move to the next base, or back to the base they just stepped away from. The ball is pitched and hit into the air close to the fence in the middle of the field (a deep **sacrifice fly ball** to center).

Strategy #5:

Assuming both runners are fairly quick, they both head back to the bases they came from and wait for a fielder to catch it or for the ball to hit the ground (base runners are **tagging up**). As soon as one of these two actions happens, both runners take off to the next base hoping to beat the throw and tag by the defense.

If the runner on first is of average or slow speed, he might not try to make it to second. The reason is the outfielder doesn't have as far a throw to second as to third and, therefore, has a better chance of getting out the base runner going to second.

STRATEGY

Batter hits a fly ball deep into the outfield.

STRATEGY

The strength of the outfielder's arm also plays into this decision. If he isn't very strong and/or accurate with his throws, the runner will probably take a chance and run to second.

If the fielder catches the ball, the defense has to tag the advancing runners out; but if the runners don't tag up, they have only to step on the original base with the ball in hand to get the runner out.

Situation #6:

A similar situation is in place as the previous one, except this time runners are on first and second with two outs in the inning. As soon as the ball is hit, without waiting to see if the ball is hit on the ground (grounder) or in the air (fly ball), they take off running toward the next base ("runners are going").

Strategy #6:

Since there are two outs, there's no reason for the base runner to worry about **tagging up** if it is a fly ball. If the defense catches the ball in the air, the batter is out, the inning over, and the runners are no longer eligible to advance on the bases to score.

The only thing the offense can hope for is that the out-fielder will not catch the fly ball, so they can advance around the bases. If this happens, the guy on second has a good opportunity to score because he is probably already at third base by the time the ball is caught.

STRATEGY

If the batter hits a grounder with two outs, the defense has to effectively field a ground ball and throw one of the runners out to end the inning, stopping the runners from advancing around the bases. Because grounders can sometimes get by the infielders, the runners want to advance around the bases as quickly as possible, hoping to beat any defensive plays. Running when the ball is hit helps them get this advantage. Also when a ground ball is hit, if a runner touches home plate before the final out of the inning is made, the run counts.

STRATEGY

Offensive Moves

Batting

Situation #1:

There are runners on first or second base, less than two outs in the inning and the hitter knocks the pitch down into the ground several feet in front of him (a **bunt**).

Strategy #1:

The manager wants to lessen the probability of the batter hitting into a double or triple play (two or three outs on one hit) to end the inning; he wants to move the base runners into a better position to score. A good bunt will only allow the defense to get a runner or the batter out, not both; a poor bunt could result in a double play or runners not being able to advance. So the manager calls this play only when he knows the hitter can bunt well.

Batter bunts the ball.

STRATEGY

A good bunt by the hitter will roll or bounce about 20 to 30 feet toward left field, so the third baseman has to make the defensive play. By doing this, the offense forces the out at first because that is the easier play (a **sacrifice bunt** by the hitter); or makes it a foot race between the shortstop and base runner to third base. If the defense tries to get out the **lead runner** (the guy on second), the shortstop will move over toward third base while the third baseman moves up toward the batter to play defense on the bunted ball.

Situation #2:

The bases are empty. A faster player is up at bat but has not been hitting well recently or has a poor batting average against the current pitcher. The coach tells him to bunt.

Strategy #2:

The reason managers use the bunt in this case is because it gives the batter a chance of outrunning a throw to first. Since the defense is not expecting a bunt, they are playing deeper in the infield (closer to the outfielders). Also, a defensive infielder must run toward home plate to field a bunt, then turn and make a good throw to first base for an out; alternatively a grounder or pop fly can be handled fairly easily for the out.

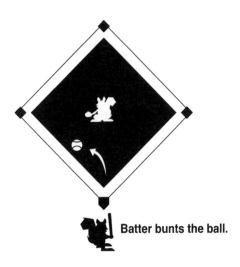

Batter bunts the ball.

Situation #3:

It is late in a close game with runners on base (offensive players on first, second, and/or third). The pitcher is up to bat in the batting order. The manager tells the umpire he's substituting a **pinch-hitter** for the pitcher.

Strategy #3:

Typically pitchers are not strong hitters. A manager puts in a pinch-hitter when the odds are better that the substitute batter will advance the runners and avoid an out.

When that half of the inning is over and the team who substituted the pinch-hitter takes the field on defense (unless it already won the game in the 9th inning), the manager typically submits additional substitutions with the umpire. The pinch-hitter brought in is rarely a pitcher, so the manager typically moves the pinch-hitter to another defensive position (remember, he substituted for the pitcher), takes that displaced defensive player out of the game, and then brings in a new pitcher from the **bullpen**.

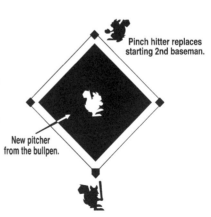

Pinch hitter replaces starting 2nd baseman.

New pitcher from the bullpen.

STRATEGY

Defensive Moves

Pitching

Situation #1:

The pitcher, catcher, and coaches decide what type of pitch to throw each batter, based on the count and game situation.

Strategy #1:

Managers, catchers, and pitchers look at the hitters' stats (see *"Water Cooler Stats"*) to see their batting percentages for certain pitches. They also look at how a batter stands at the plate: crowding it, open stance, closed stance, etc. Another key stat is the hitter's batting average against right-handed versus left-handed pitchers. If the guy is a **switch hitter** (can effectively hit from either side of the plate), the coaches determine what pitches will work better against him when he hits right-handed versus left-handed. Lastly, if runners are on base, a certain pitch might be thrown to try to force the batter to hit into a **double play** or fly out. The bottom line is the pitcher doesn't just toss a fastball when he feels like it.

STRATEGY

Situation #2:

The batter is behind in the count (e.g., one ball and two strikes [1–2] or no balls and two strikes [0–2]).

Strategy #2:

The pitcher typically throws a couple of waste balls (not even close to the **strike zone**), hoping to get the batter to strikeout. If the batter makes contact with the ball, he probably won't hit in fair territory. The pitcher also will take the opportunity to set up the batter by throwing several similar pitches in a row, then come back on a key pitch and throw a completely different pitch. For example, a batter is pitched three low fastballs in a row then thrown a change-up (slow pitch). He will probably swing early and miss the ball for the third strike.

Sport's Shorts

The "7th Inning Stretch" dates back to 1869 when Harry Wright of the Cincinnati Red Stockings noticed fans tended to get up and move about during the middle of the seventh inning. The stretch became a tradition, accompanied by everyone singing the chorus of "Take Me Out to the Ball Game."

STRATEGY

Situation #3:

The batter is ahead in the count (e.g., two balls and no strikes [2–0] or three balls and one strike [3–1]), with a runner on second.

Strategy #3:

The batter usually takes a pitch if the count is 3–1, meaning he won't swing at it even if he thinks it will be in the strike zone. So the pitcher tries to throw something he thinks the batter will have trouble hitting yet still be in the strike zone. The pitcher doesn't want to give up a walk (if there are three balls in the pitch count). Nor does he want to serve up an easily hit pitch, because the batter might just decide to swing and take it out of the park (a home run). But with the runner on second, he would rather walk the hitter and give his team a chance for a **force-out** instead of giving up a hit, which could turn into a run.

> ### *Sport's Shorts*
>
> How can a player go 0–4 in a game and still score three runs? If there are runners on base, three runs could have scored on an error, walk, and sacrifice fly. There are other combinations, but this shows statistics alone don't tell the whole story.

Situation #4:

It's late in a close game and the manager brings in a **relief pitcher** to face just one hitter, then brings in another relief pitcher.

Strategy #4:

The manager is trying to match his pitchers effectively against the upcoming hitters. He might bring in a **reliever** who pitches left-handed, to face a left-handed batter. By doing this, the defensive manager is counting on the batter actually batting. However, the offensive manager may negate the strategy by putting in a **pinch hitter** who bats right-handed. Most of the time, you'll see pitching changes based on the batting style of the next three hitters instead of just one. If two of the next three batters are right-handed, the relief pitcher will probably be right-handed. There are many variations based on the statistics teams keep, but understand there is a method to their madness.

STRATEGY

Sport's Shorts

Did you know professional baseball began keeping stats in 1876, the year the National League was formed?

Situation #5:

Sometimes a manager brings in a relief pitcher who will get **shelled** (no matter what he pitches, the offensive team keeps getting hits and scoring on him) by the first several hitters. So the manager needs to bring in another reliever earlier in the game than planned. In this situation, several defensive players and coaches take turns going out to the mound and talking to the current pitcher.

Strategy #5:

This is not a pep talk by half the team (as it may seem). Rather it is a stall tactic to give the next relief pitcher time to warm up. It takes more than eight pitches for a pitcher to get warmed up (all that are allowed once he enters the game, unless he's replacing an injured pitcher).

To give him more time, the defense uses delay tactics. The catcher and some of the infielders may go out and talk to the pitcher. He throws a couple of pitches. Then the pitching coach comes out and talks to the guy. He throws another pitch or two. Finally, the manager comes out. The umpire only allows a limited amount of time for conversing and sometimes will walk to the mound to break up the meeting.

Situation #6:

A runner who has a reputation for stealing bases is on base. Instead of a full **windup** (arms above his head and a high kick prior to throwing the ball), the pitcher pitches out of the **stretch** (much less movement before the pitch).

Strategy #6:

He is trying to minimize his movement and the amount of time it takes to deliver the pitch. He wants to get the ball quickly from his hand to the catcher, then on to the covering baseman. Also, for as long as possible during his delivery, he wants to hide whether he is pitching or throwing the ball to the runner's base.

Full Windup   **The Stretch**

STRATEGY

Defensive Moves

Managing the Bases

Situation #1:

Runners are on second and third with less than two outs. The defense decides to pitch the hitter four balls in a row (intentional walk), which loads the bases as the hitter moves to first base.

Strategy #1:

This puts a **force play** opportunity on any base. That means if the ball is hit on the ground, all the runners have to advance and the defensive player only has to touch any of the bases (usually with a foot) with the ball in their hand for an out. This creates an opportunity for a double or triple play by allowing the defense to touch a base and quickly throw the ball to another base for multiple outs.

2nd baseman catches
ball. He throws it to shortstop
covering 2nd who touches the
base and turns to throw the
runner out at 3rd.

STRATEGY

If the bases weren't loaded and a **grounder** is fielded, the defense would probably only get the hitter out at first, since the base runners probably wouldn't try to advance, or they got a good jump leaving the defense little chance of an out.

Situation #2:

It's late in a close game with an open base (bases aren't loaded). The defense **intentionally walks** a good hitter to put him on first base.

Strategy #2:

The coaches don't want to take a chance that the batter will get a hit or home run, scoring the base runner(s). They intentionally walk him, so they can pitch to the next batter whom isn't as likely to hit safely (getting on base without an out). The offense may counter this move by putting in a good **pinch hitter**, instead of the next batter listed in the lineup, hoping he can score one run or more.

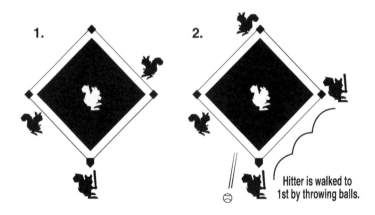

Hitter is walked to 1st by throwing balls.

Situation #3:

It's late in a close game with an open base (bases aren't loaded). The defense intentionally walks the next hitter to put him on first base. This hitter has a mediocre batting average overall, but the defensive coach knows he is hitting about .500 (that is, he records a hit half the time he bats) against the current pitcher.

Strategy #3:

To eliminate the chance that this hitter will have a successful at-bat, without having to take out an otherwise effective pitcher, the manager has his team pitch around (intentionally walk) the hitter, hoping to get the next batter(s) out.

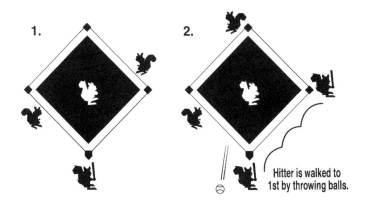

Hitter is walked to 1st by throwing balls.

Situation #4:

When each new batter comes to the plate, the defensive players move in/out or right/left in their coverage areas.

Strategy #4:

Before each series, the defense studies the tendencies of each hitter on a team. Some players are long-ball hitters, some hit short, some pull the ball (e.g., right-handers hit toward the left side of the field), and others tend to bunt often, etc. Then they make adjustments, depending on the game situation (as discussed in the other Situation/Strategy examples). For example, a runner is on first and the pitcher is up to bat. The defense (infield and outfield) will probably move in expecting a bunt.

STRATEGY

Sport's Shorts

There's an old trick, circa the late 1800s, used to catch base runners. The baseman covering the runner's bag has the ball and pretends to throw it back to the pitcher. In actuality, he still has the ball in his hand or glove; he will wait until the runner takes a lead off the base to tag him out. The pitcher has to play his part by acting like he has caught the ball.

Situation #5:

A runner is on base (usually first). The pitcher throws several balls to the baseman to try and tag the runner when he strays from the base.

Strategy #5:

The pitcher does this most often when a known base stealer is on a bag, so he won't get a big lead toward the next base. The *down side* to keeping the runner close to the base is that the pitcher can't focus solely on making the correct pitches to the hitter and could make a mistake when throwing to the base or delivering the next pitch. The *up side* is the pitcher might catch the base runner too far off base and the baseman tags him out before he can get back safely.

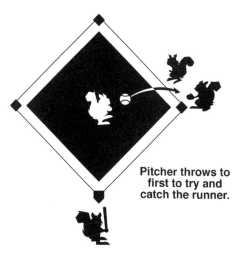

Pitcher throws to first to try and catch the runner.

STRATEGY

Situation #6:

Runners are on first and second with less than two outs. The batter hits a ground ball to an infielder. The base runner takes off and runs full-steam to third base. The infielder looks at third to see if he can beat the runner with the throw. If not, he will throw to first.

Strategy #6:

In situations like this, the defense always tries to get the **lead runner** (the man running from second to third) out or the trailing runner. By throwing out the lead runner, the easy scoring threat is removed from third base. If the defense throws out the trailing runner, then one runner is out of scoring position and it sets up the offense for a double play at first and second during the next at-bat. If there is no play on the base runners (the fielder doesn't think he can throw either out) the fielder wants to get at least one out, which means throwing to first.

STRATEGY

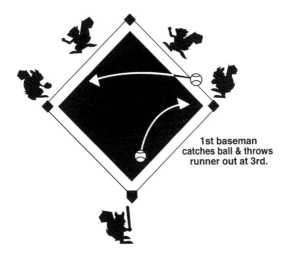

1st baseman
catches ball & throws
runner out at 3rd.

STRATEGY

The batter is the last option, because the defense has more time to get the ball to first base for an out. The batter starts from an awkward position by following through on his swing. Also, he has to run the full 90 feet so he is an easier out. Base runners typically move toward the next base before the ball is hit (90 feet minus lead distance), which gives them more momentum and less distance to travel during the same time frame.

Water Cooler Stats

Statistics are used to make decisions on lineup, starting pitcher, pinch-hitters, relief pitchers, and any number of other strategic moves related to managing a game. There are probably more stats kept in baseball than any other sport. It wouldn't be a surprise if they kept stats on the average number of times the opposing team's lead off hitter adjusts his equipment before stepping into the **batter's box**.

If you go to www.MLB.com and click on their "Stats" tab, you will see a list of statistics for each player. You will also find some of these listed in **box scores**, and other stats reported in your local paper.

Hitting and Fielding Stats

• **2B** (Doubles) – Number of doubles hit by a player.

• **3B** (Triples) – Number of triples hit by a player.

• **AB** (At-Bats) – The number of at-bats a hitter has, with the exception of **sacrifice** hits, walks, hit by pitches, and obstructions.

• **AVG** (Batting Average) $= \dfrac{\text{number of hits}}{\text{number of at-bats}}$

• **BB** (Bases on Balls) $= \dfrac{\text{number of walks}}{\text{number of at-bats}}$

- **CS** (Caught Stealing) – Number of times a base runner was caught stealing.

- **E** (Errors) – When a fielder should have made a play on a fair ball but made a mistake in catching or throwing as determined by official scorekeepers.

- **FPCT** (Fielding Percentage) $= \dfrac{\text{fielder outs + assists}}{\text{outs + assists + errors}}$

- **G** (Games Played) – Number of games played as a starter or substitute, out of a possible 162 games played in a full regular season.

- **H** (Hits) – Number of times a batter gets on base safely by hitting the ball in fair territory and without an error by the defense or a ruled **fielder's choice**.

- **HBP** (Hit By Pitch) – Number of times a batter is hit by a pitch.

- **HR** (Home Runs) – Number of home runs hit by a player.

- **HR Ratio** (Home Run Ratio) $= \dfrac{\text{number of at-bats}}{\text{home runs}}$

- **INN** (Innings) – Number of innings played on defense, with each out counting one-third of an inning.

- **OBP** (On Base %) $= \dfrac{(\text{hits + walks + hit by pitches})}{(\text{walks + hit by pitches + at-bats + \textbf{sacrifice} flies})}$

STATS

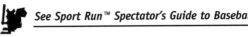

- **R** (Runs) – Number of times a player scores.

- **RBI** (Runs Batted In) – Number of runs scored during a player's single at-bat, which can be from players running in from other bases or from scoring himself. If a runner scores on a defensive error and would not have scored otherwise, it is not counted as a RBI.

- **SB** (Stolen Bases) $= \dfrac{\text{number of stolen bases}}{\text{number of total stolen bases attempted}}$

- **SF** (Sacrifice Flies) – Number of times a batter hits a sacrifice fly in a season.

- **SLG** (Slugging Percentage) $= \dfrac{\text{total number of bases}}{\text{number of at-bats}}$

- **SO** (Strikeouts) $= \dfrac{\text{number of at-bats}}{\text{strikeouts}}$

- **TB** (Total Bases) – Number of bases accumulated. It is calculated by adding all the bases a player reaches safely with 1st base equaling one, 2nd base equaling two, 3rd base equaling three, and home plate equaling four.

Pitching Stats

- **BB** (Base on Balls) – Number of walks issued by a pitcher.

STATS

- **ER** (Earned Runs) – Number of scores allowed by a pitcher without an error.

- **ERA** (Earned Run Average) $=$ $\dfrac{\text{earned runs allowed} \times 9}{\text{total number of innings pitched}}$

- **G** (Games) – Number of times a pitcher plays a full or partial game.

- **GS** (Games Started) – Number of times a pitcher starts a game.

- **H** (Hits) – Number of hits pitcher gives up.

- **Hld** (Holds) – Earned when a relief pitcher enters a game in a save situation, records at least one out, and leaves the game without having given up the lead.

- **HR** (Home Runs) – Number of home runs hit against the pitcher.

- **IP** (Innings Pitched) – Number of innings pitched. Innings are divided into thirds with each out equaling 1/3. For example, a pitcher that has pitched a full game (9) and was relieved after 6 innings and one out (6 1/3) in his next start has pitched 15 1/3 innings.

- **L** (Loss) – Pitcher is charged with a loss if his team is behind when he leaves the game, even if runs are scored afterward. To be a loss, his team must lose by having fewer runs batted in and without tying or taking the lead in the score.

STATS

- **R** (Runs) – Number of runs a pitcher gives up.

- **SO** (Strikeouts) – Number of strikeouts the pitcher records.

- **SV** (Saves) – A relief pitcher who finishes a winning game and either (a) pitches at least one inning with the lead but no more than a three-run lead when entering; (b) comes into the game with the potential tying-run either at-bat, on-deck, or on base; (c) pitches at least three innings.

- **SVO** (Save Opportunities) – A relief pitcher comes into a game with a lead of three runs or less with the potential tying run on base, at-bat, or coming up as the next batter.

- **W** (Win) – The starting pitcher completes at least five innings, and the team maintains a lead that was set up when he left the game.

Team Stats

- **W-L** (Won-Lost Percentage) $= \dfrac{\text{number of games won}}{\text{number of games completed}}$

- **GB** (Games Behind) $= \dfrac{(\text{leader's total wins} - \text{trailer's total wins}) + (\text{leader's total losses} - \text{trailer's total losses})}{2}$

- Magic Number – Number of games needed to clinch the division title, calculated by subtracting the number of games ahead of the second-place team from the total number of games left to play in the season, then add 1.

As you may have noticed, a few stats use the same abbreviation for different actions. For example, *HR* means the number of home runs hit by a batter and the number given up by a pitcher. To keep it straight, look to see where in the stats area (offensive or defensive) the abbreviation is being used.

Below is an example of offensive stats, so you can see Dunn has hit 6 *home runs* thus far in the season.

PLAYER	TEAM	POS	G	AB	R	H	2B	3B	HR	RBI	TB	BB	SO	SB	CS	OBP	SLG	AVG
A RODRIGUEZ	TEX	88	16	63	13	19	3	0	7	12	43	6	18	1	0	0.380	0.683	.302
J BAGWELL	HOU	1B	16	62	11	23	4	0	7	11	48	9	3	1	1	0.466	0.774	.371
A DUNN	CIN	OF	15	51	10	11	1	0	6	11	30	8	21	0	1	0.333	0.588	.216
A KEARNS	CIN	OF	16	52	12	14	0	0	6	12	32	11	12	0	1	0.415	0.615	.269
H BLALOCK	TEX	3B	13	52	10	22	1	0	5	9	38	4	5	0	1	0.464	0.731	.423

STATS

Below is an example of pitching stats, so you can see Maddux has given up 7 *home runs* thus far in the season.

PLAYER	TEAM	W	L	ERA	G	GS	SV	SVO	IP	H	R	ER	HR	BB	SO
G MADDUX	ATL	1	3	8.27	4	4	0	0	20	31	25	19	7	6	17
C GEORGE	KC	2	1	5.94	3	3	0	0	16	19	11	11	6	6	8
L JENSEN	SF	0	0	15.95	2	2	0	0	7	15	13	13	6	2	3
J MANZANILLO	CIN	0	2	11.17	8	0	0	1	9	19	17	12	6	3	12
K APPIER	ANA	1	2	6.61	3	3	0	0	16	19	12	12	5	8	10

STATS

Baseball Lingo

40/40 Club – A player hits 40 **home runs** and has 40 **stolen bases** in a season. This is not really a club, but rather a feat that baseball's statisticians identified as unique after Jose Canseco did it in 1988. There are currently only two other players in this elite "club"– Alex Rodriguez and Barry Bonds.

Ace – A dominant and well-respected pitcher who can strike out good hitters and win many games for his team.

Appeal – When a team disagrees with a call, in certain situations they can ask another umpire to make a call, given his vantage point on the field. If play continues, the team cannot go back and appeal an earlier play.

At-bat – This is each time a hitter comes to the plate during a game and either gets a hit, strikes out, or hits into an out.

Backstop – The protective wall behind home plate that protects people in the stands from foul balls, wild pitches, and errant throws.

Bag – Another name for **base**. It's easy to remember because bases are actually canvas bags stuffed with various types of soft material.

TERMS

Balk – The pitcher starts his throwing motion toward home plate, then turns and instead throws to one of the three bases. If this foul is called by an umpire, the runners advance one base. If the pitcher does not come to a complete stop with his throwing hand in his glove in front of his chest, before releasing the pitch, it is a *balk*. This is a very subjective call; you don't see it often in a season. To avoid a balk, before releasing the ball, the pitcher must step toward the base to which he is throwing.

Ball – The round white leather object being thrown around on the field. Also, a pitch thrown outside the **strike zone** at which the batter doesn't swing.

Base – One of the three white, square canvas bags on the playing field, which base runners must touch in order to score a run. Also called **Bag** and **Base Pad**.

Baseline – An imaginary space surrounding the white lines that run between all of the bases; it is three feet on each side of the line. Umpires are liberal with the range when players are running the bases and less forgiving when caught in a **run down**.

Base Pad – Another name for **base**.

Base Runner – The offensive player on first, second, or third base.

Batter – The offensive player with the bat in his hand at home plate who tries to hit the ball or get on base by drawing a **walk**.

Batter's Box – The white rectangles on either side of home plate, where the batter stands.

Batting Order – A list of a team's batters, showing the position each will hit in the **at-bat** rotation during a game.

Bigs – Slang for the major league playing level (see **MLB**) versus the **farm system**. When a player or coach is promoted from a farm team to the major league club, he's "Going to the *Bigs*." Also called the **Show**.

Blue – Slang term for umpires (one of the nicer terms). For example, "Hey, *Blue*, you call that a strike?!"

Bottom of the Inning – The second half of an **inning** when the home team is up to bat.

Bottom of the Order – The last four hitters in a team's lineup (sixth through ninth spots).

Box Scores – The statistical summary for a game, showing information such as the score by inning, pitching information, and hitting statistics.

Boys of Summer – A nickname for baseball players.

TERMS

Bullpen – Area where relief pitchers warm up during a game. Also, the staff of relief pitchers. The saying, "He's going to his *bullpen* early," means early in the game the manager is substituting the starter with a relief pitcher.

Bunt – The batter moves one of his hands up the shaft of the bat, then brings it down off his shoulder, positioning the bat parallel to the ground. The goal is to knock the pitch down, making it bounce or roll 20 to 30 feet in front of the plate toward either first or third base while staying fair.

Catcher – The defensive player that squats behind home plate to catch the pitches that are thrown. He is also responsible for giving the pitcher signals, throwing out offensive players who try to steal a base, and performing defensive duties in guarding home plate.

Change-up – A slow pitch (in MLB typically it's about 80 mph), that looks like a **fastball**. It is intended to throw hitters off and entice them into swinging too soon at the pitch.

Check Swing – When a batter begins his swinging motion on a pitch, but stops before getting half way through the entire swinging motion. This does not count as a swinging strike against the hitter, but the umpire could still call a strike if the pitch was in the **strike zone**.

Chin Music – Slang for a pitch thrown high and inside near the batter's face. Also called a bowtie. For example, "That *chin music* should stop the batter from crowding the plate."

Cleanup Hitter – Player who usually bats fourth in the batting order and is a home-run type of hitter. This batting position gets its name from the fact that three hitters have already hit; if any or all got on base he tries to "clean them off" by hitting a home run or getting a big hit.

Climbing the Ladder – When a fielder jumps up high in the air and stretches skyward to catch a ball in play.

Closer – The **ace** relief pitcher out of the **bullpen**. He is put in to finish a close game and to strive to get a save or win. There can be several relief pitchers in a game between the starter and *closer*. If the game is out of hand, the manager won't tire a closer's arm; instead he will use another reliever.

Complete Shutout – The starting pitcher pitches an entire game and doesn't allow any runs to be scored by the opposing team.

Count – The number of balls (always listed first) and strikes (always listed second) against the current hitter. For example, 2–1 means there are two balls and one strike against the hitter.

TERMS

Curve Ball – A pitch with enough spin to make it break down and to the left or right depending on with which hand the player pitches; right-handers break left, and vice versa.

Cut-off Man – Defensive player who takes a throw from an outfielder and relays it to a player near the infield area. This guy is necessary because most outfielders don't have the arm strength to make an accurate throw to all of the bases for a potential out.

Defense – The team on the field and pitching.

Designated Hitter – Found only in American League home games. An additional player is used to hit in place of the pitcher in the batting order and, consequently, does not play defense during the game in this role.

Dinger – Slang for a home run. For example, "That ball is out of here! He just hit his second *dinger* of the day!"

Disabled List (DL) – When a player is injured and can't perform, then teams will designate him to the list. During this time, they can add another player to the roster who is typically from the team's AAA affiliate.

Double – A hit that allows the batter to get onto second base without an error by the defense.

Doubleheader – Two teams play two games in one day, in the afternoon and evening.

TERMS

Double Play – Two outs take place on a single hit.

Double Switch – Two players are substituted at once.

Doughnut – A round weight, in the shape of that sinful pastry. Used by batters to loosen up before hitting. Mounted by sliding over the smaller end of the bat.

Drawing a Pass – A batter is hitting well, or is known for his hitting ability. A pitcher intentionally walks the batter to avoid giving up a costly hit, run, or home run. When this happens, the batter is said to have *drawn a pass*.

Dugout – Area on either side of the field where the teams and coaches sit during a game. The home team is in one; the visiting team is in the other.

Fair Ball – A ball struck by the batter that lands inside the white foul lines anywhere on the field of play or over the outfield fence.

Fall Classic – Another name for the **World Series**.

Farm System – The **minor leagues** located in many towns around North America. They provide a training ground for inexperienced, aspiring, and rehabbing players who are trying for a chance at the major league level.

Fastball – The pitcher throws the ball with as much velocity and control as possible and little spin movement.

TERMS

Typically, MLB pitchers throw fastballs in the 90⁺ mph range.

Fielder's Choice – One or more runners are on base. The batter hits a ground ball. The defensive fielder chooses to try and get a base runner out, instead of the batter running to first. If the inning isn't over after the out(s) are recorded, the base runner is said to have reached base "on a *fielder's choice*."

Fly Ball – The batter hits the ball high in the air, out of the infield area either in fair or foul territory. A *fly out* is when that ball is caught in the air by a defender.

Force Play (also see **Fielder's Choice**) – A ground ball is hit in fair territory. Any runners on a base, with all the bases behind them loaded, have to take the next base. In this situation, the infielders need to touch only the base with the ball in their hand for the advancing runner to be out. For example, runners are on first and second. The batter hits a ground ball to the shortstop. The *force plays* are on first, second, and third and could result in a double or triple play.

Foul Ball – A ball struck by the batter and lands outside the white foul lines either on the field or in the stands. This includes balls that land behind the **batter's box**.

Foul Pole – The tall yellow poles rising up out of the outfield fence. The foul line is extended from the field vertically up into the air. If a ball hits a yellow pole, it is called a **fair ball**.

Free Pass – Slang for a **walk**. For example, "The pitcher just issued his second *free pass* in this inning to load the bases."

Full Count – Three balls and two strikes are against the hitter (3–2). It's called this because if the hitter gets either another strike or ball called against him he will be out or walked, respectively, which ends the **at-bat**.

Game – Nine innings of play, unless the umpire calls the game after five full innings due to bad weather or other circumstances that endanger the players and coaches. Or, if the game is tied after regulation play, the contest is finally won after extra innings.

Grand Slam – A home run hit when the bases are loaded (runners on first, second, and third), which scores four runs.

Green Monster – A 37-foot-high wall painted green. It stands as the left field fence in Boston's Fenway Park.

Grounder – A ball hits the ground bouncing or rolling, and can be either fair or foul.

Ground-Rule Double – A **fly ball** hits in fair territory on the field of play, then bounces over the outfield fence. The runners can advance only two bases. It is scored as a **double** in the statistics.

TERMS

Heat – Slang term for a good **fastball**. For example, "The batters can't handle his *heat* today." Sometimes you will hear *high heat*, which is a fastball thrown up around the batter's chest area.

Hit – The ball lands in fair territory (not caught in the air by the defense). The batter makes it safely onto base without a defensive error.

Hit-and-Run – An offensive play usually called when there's a runner on base with fewer than two outs and the batter gets ahead in the count. The batter swings at the next pitch. The **lead runner** starts running toward the next base at the point when the pitcher begins his throwing motion.

Hitter – A batter.

Home Plate – The flat rubber base that the catcher and umpire squat behind and has to be touched to score a run.

Home Run – Can be **"in-the-park"** (ball lands in fair territory) or "out of the park" (goes over the fence in fair territory). To score, the runner has to touch all three bases, finishing with home plate.

Hot Corner – Slang for **third base**. For example, "What a catch by the third baseman! That's why they put him on the *hot corner*."

Infield – The dirt and turf area between the foul lines where the bases and **pitcher's mound** are located. Also the group of defenders positioned in that area (first, second, and third basemen, and shortstop).

Infielder – A defensive player (first, second, third baseman, or shortstop) who guards the bases. Usually positioned around the dirt area of the field between the pitcher and outfielders.

Infield Fly Rule – The batter pops a fair ball into the air and the ball doesn't fly beyond the infield, the umpire calls the *infield fly rule*. The batter is automatically called out, whether the ball is caught or not, and the runners cannot advance. This rule was put into place to prevent a defensive player from purposefully missing a fly ball and getting an easy double or triple play. Contrast this to a **fly ball** to the outfield where a runner may tag up and run after the fielder catches the ball.

Inherited Runners – Runners on base when a relief pitcher comes into the game.

Inning – Both the home and away teams complete their at-bats by recording three outs each.

Intentional Walk – The defense decides they don't want to take a chance that the current batter will score one or more runs (by hitting a home run or hitting a ball that scores runners on base). The pitcher purposefully throws

TERMS

four balls outside of the **batter's box**. By doing this, they ensure the batter won't be able to swing at the pitch, and the runners and batter will advance only one base.

In-the-park Home Run – A batter hits the ball inside of the outfield fence and in fair play. He is able to run all of the bases and score with that one hit.

Juice – Slang term with a couple of different meanings: (a) A high speed pitch, or (b) Steroids players inject to enhance their performance. For example, "This guy seems like a different pitcher after last year's perform-ance, with the *juice* he has on that ball," or "He is so muscular. Do you think he is on the *juice*?"

K – Scoring symbol for a **strikeout**. Sometimes you will see fans in the stands flashing big signs with the letter *K* on it, which they hang up on a rail for each strikeout recorded by the current pitcher.

Lead-off Hitter – The player who hits first in the **batting order** during a game.

Lead Runner – The base runner on the base closest to home when a ball is hit. He's the biggest threat to score, so the defensive tactic is to try get the *lead runner* out first.

Line Drive – A hard hit fly ball that looks like it is mov-ing almost parallel to the ground until it lands or is caught.

TERMS

Manager – The head coach of a team. He is responsible for overall team management during a game (e.g., line-ups, pitching changes, defensive shifts in the field, and substitutions).

Meat of the Order – The third through the fifth hitters in a batting lineup.

Middle Reliever – A relief pitcher who typically comes into a game in the fifth or sixth inning and pitches any-where from one at-bat to several innings before being replaced by another reliever or **closer**.

Minor Leagues – The leagues teams use to develop or rehab players for the major league team affiliate. Designated AAA, AA, A, and Rookie. AAA showcases the most talented pool of players out of all these leagues.

MLB (Major League Baseball) – The official governing entity of the largest professional baseball organization in the United States and Canada.

No-hitter – A starting pitcher throws for the entire game and doesn't allow the opposing team to get a single hit.

Offense – The team currently batting.

Official Scorer – The person who determines the correct data for inclusion in the official MLB stats, such as errors, hits, and saves.

TERMS

Ohfer – A slang term describing when someone doesn't get a hit during a game or is hitless against another team. For example, if a player has no hits with five at-bats in a game, you might say, "He was *ohfer* in last night's game."

On-deck Circle – The white circle next to the **dugout** where the next batter (player on-deck) warms up.

Opening Day – The first date a regular season game is played each year in MLB; and the first date each club plays their first game of the regular season. Also, the first game played at home by each team, as in *Opening Day* at Wrigley Field. These games are usually at the end of March or beginning of April.

Out – A player on offense is beaten on a play and forced to leave the field. For example, the batter's ball is caught in the air, a runner is tagged before touching a base, or a batter has three strikes called against him.

Outfield – Area bordered by the outfield fence, the infield, and the foul lines. Also, the team of defenders covering that area: left, center, and right fielders.

Outfielders – Defensive players out in the grassy area positioned between the infielders and outfield wall (left, right, and center fielders).

Passed Ball – A pitch is deemed within reach of the catcher, but the pitch goes past him because of a failed play on the ball. This is statistically recorded as an error only if the batter reaches first base or a runner advances a base because of the errant throw.

Pen – Area where relief pitchers warm up (or the staff of relief pitchers). Also see **bullpen**.

Perfect Game – When a team doesn't allow a batter from the opposing team to reach first base. This means there are no walks, errors, hit batters or hits allowed by the winning team. The pitcher is credited with a perfect game because he does most of the work. For example, "Johnson pitched a *perfect game* today."

Pickoff – A base runner is tagged out by the defense before he gets safely to a base.

Pinch Hitter – Substitute for another player on his own team in the batting order. Takes the exiting player's position on defense.

Pinch Runner – Substitute for another player on his own team who is on a base, but new runner cannot be in the lineup at the time of substitution. Takes the exiting player's position in the batting order and on defense.

Pitch – The pitcher throws the ball to the catcher with no time or a **balk** called prior to the release.

TERMS

Pitch Count – Number of official pitches a pitcher throws in a game.

Pitcher – The defensive guy on the mound in the middle of the infield who throws pitches in a game.

Pitcher's Mound – The raised dirt area in the middle of the infield with the white rubber strip on top of it.

Pitchout – A pitcher intentionally throws a pitch well outside the **strike zone** so the batter will not be able to make contact with the ball. Subsequently called a ball by the umpire. Also see **Intentional Walk**.

Postseason Games – The playoffs and **World Series**.

Putout – A defensive player gets an offensive player out in any manner. Also see **out**.

Reliever (or *Relief Pitcher*) – Pitchers who come in from the **bullpen** when the starting pitcher has been taken out of the game or is injured.

Rope – Slang for a **line drive**. For example, "The shortstop had no chance to make a play on that *rope* to center field."

Roster – The players on a baseball team.

Rubber Game – The third game in a three-game series when each team has won one each.

TERMS

Run – A player successfully tags all four bases with less than three outs on his team in an inning.

Run Down – The ball is in play and a base runner is caught between bases with defenders on either side trying to tag him out. The defender with the ball chases the runner toward one of the bases. As he gets close to it, the player with the ball tosses it to his teammate in front of the base. They continue this chasing and tossing the ball back and forth until they tag the runner out or he safely makes it to a base.

Sacrifice (SAC) – A batter forgoes his opportunity to reach base safely in order to advance a base runner. He does this by hitting the ball in an area that only provides the defense with the opportunity to get the hitter out. Commonly you will see *sacrifice bunts* and *flies* (fly balls to the outfield).

Safe – An offensive player advances around the base pads or returns to a base without being tagged out by a defensive player.

Save – A relief pitcher comes into a game in which his team is ahead and wins the game, but he doesn't get credit for a win by the official scorer.

Shelled – A pitcher just doesn't have his "mojo" going that day and the batters are hitting everything he tries to

TERMS

throw. For example, "We're seeing some stall tactics, because the **skipper** didn't think his pitcher would get *shelled* like that."

Show – The major-league playing level. For example, "Since the White Sox catcher got hurt yesterday, Sam Jones in AAA is going to the *Show*." Also see **Bigs**.

Single – A hit that allows the batter to get to first base without an error on the defense.

Skipper – Slang for **manager**. For example, "The *skipper* is going out to the mound to pull his ace."

Southpaw – Slang for a left-handed pitcher. For example, "The *southpaw* comes into the game in relief of the starting pitcher."

Spring Training – Practice games that last the month of March each year in Arizona and Florida. Used to get players back into game form and evaluate new players who are trying to make the regular season **roster**.

Squeeze Play – A runner is on third. The batter tries to get him home by bunting. The runner at third waits until the ball is successfully hit before taking off for home plate. A *suicide squeeze* is when the runner takes off from the base at some point during the pitching sequence but before the ball is hit. It's called a suicide because, if the batter misses the ball, the catcher is in a great position to tag the runner out easily.

Steal – A **base runner** tries to advance from one base to another without the ball being hit. This is commonly started at some point during the pitching motion.

Stolen Base – A successful **steal**.

Stretch – A modified **windup** motion by the pitcher. Typically used when runners are on base. By shortening and/or increasing the speed of his motions, the pitcher can somewhat disguise the throw to first or home. Also, he gets rid of the ball quicker to home plate; so if the base runner tries to steal, the catcher has a better chance of throwing him out.

Strike – When the batter swings and misses, or doesn't swing, and the umpire determines that the ball crossed the plate in the **strike zone**. A *strike* is also called if the batter hits the ball into foul territory with less than two strikes against him.

Strike Count – The number of strikes against a batter in a single **at-bat** (also see **count**).

Strikeout – The batter gets three strikes against him (an out) and his **at-bat** is complete.

TERMS

Strike Zone – The area around home plate considered a strike by the umpire. An imaginary box where the top is even with the chest of the batter, the bottom with his knees, and the sides extend up from home plate.

Striking Out Looking – The pitcher throws a strike as called by the umpire. With two strikes already against him, the batter doesn't swing at it and is called out.

Striking Out Swinging – The batter swings and misses the ball, picking up his third strike and is out.

Sweep – A team wins all of the games in a given series or during a season against another team.

Switch Hitter – A player who can bat effectively from either side of the plate, left-handed or right-handed.

Tag – A defensive player touches a base runner (if no time-out is in effect), with the ball in his hand or in his glove, while the runner is not on base, resulting in an out.

Tagging Up – Usually runners on base take a few steps toward the next base once the pitcher has set-up to pitch the ball. If the ball is hit in the air (fly ball) and stays within fair territory in the park, the runner has to go back and remain on that base until the ball is caught or dropped by the fielder before advancing to the next one.

TERMS

If the fielder catches the ball, the runner can choose to stay on that base or try to advance to the next base. If the fielder misses the ball, the runner must advance to the next base if the bases are full behind him or if he is on first base (also see **Force Play**).

Time – Play on the field is stopped by one of the umpires. No one can score, steal, be called out, or execute any other action related to the game.

Top of the Inning – The first half of an inning when the visiting team is up to bat; sometimes called the *top half of the inning*.

Top of the Order – The first two batters in the **batting order**.

Triple – A hit allowing the batter to get to third base without an error on the defense.

Triple Play – Three outs are recorded on a single hit.

Umpires – The officials on the field who make calls related to a game.

Walk – A pitcher throws four balls before getting the batter to **strikeout** or hit the ball, so the hitter advances to first base.

TERMS

Walk-off Home Run – A home run to win the game, which is always by the home team since they are last to bat in each inning

Warning Track – The dirt area (typically six feet wide) usually around the entire field. It lets fielders know when they are getting close to the wall.

Wild Pitch – The pitcher throws the ball into the dirt with a sharp break, or way out of the **strike zone** so that it goes past the catcher. This is statistically recorded as an error only if the batter reaches first base or a runner advances a base because of the errant throw.

Win – One of the teams scores more runs than the other in an official game. Also, a statistical reference where the pitcher is awarded the game if he meets certain criteria.

Windup – The motion a pitcher goes through just before releasing the ball when throwing a pitch to home plate. With his pitching hand in his glove, he raises them at or above his head, kicks up his front leg, and sends the ball toward home plate.

World Series – MLB's championship series, held each year in October, between the National League and American League playoff winners. The first team to win four games (commonly referred to as "best of seven") is crowned champion.

Now That You're Hooked

If this Guide has whetted your appetite for baseball and you want more information, the resources listed here are recommended.

Books

- *Baseball for Dummies, 2nd Edition* by Joe Morgan, IDG Books Worldwide, Inc., 2000
- *The Complete Idiot's Guide to Baseball* by Johnny Bench, Alpha Books, 1999

Web Sites

- www.ballparksofbaseball.com–Pictures and commentary on all MLB ballparks
- www.baseballhalloffame.org–Official web site of the Baseball Hall of Fame in Cooperstown, New York
- www.baseball-links.com–Links to all kinds of baseball sites, from T-ball to the majors
- www.baseball-reference.com–Stats and history
- www.bigleaguers.com–Information on MLB players
- www.espn.com–Information on all kinds of sports with MLB links on the left-hand menu

- www.foxsports.com–Similar to ESPN site, click on the baseball icon at the top of the page

- www.mlb.com–Official web site of Major League Baseball (MLB) with links to all team sites

- www.SeeSportRun.com–For new and casual fans, containing information similar to this book, for baseball and other spectator sports

- www.sportingnews.com–Good general sports site, click on MLB links at the top of the page

- www.usatoday.com/sports/baseball/front.htm–Current baseball news published by *USA Today*

Printed Publications

- *Baseball Digest*–Baseball only
- *ESPN The Magazine*–General sports news
- *Sports Illustrated*–General sports news
- *The Sporting News*–General sports news
- *USA Today's Sports Weekly*–General sports news

Sources Used in See Sport Run Baseball Guide

- *Baseball for Dummies* by Joe Morgan
- *Sports Illustrated*, July 15–22, 2002
- *Sports Illustrated*, March 31, 2003
- *The Complete Idiot's Guide to Baseball* by Johnny Bench
- www.ballparksofbaseball.com

- www.baseball-almanac.com
- www.baseball-reference.com
- www.howstuffworks.com
- www.mlb.com

Index

Visit Sport, the See Sport Run™ mascot, at www.SeeSportRun.com where he shares his knowledge of other sports:

- Basketball
- Football
- Golf
- Ice Hockey
- Lacrosse
- Soccer

For each sport he will provide you with:

- Weekly lessons
- Current sports news
- Online glossary
- Chat rooms
- Numerous resources
- Games

While you are at the site join Sport's Club to get updates and provide feedback on the web site and books. Clothing and guides to other sports are available for purchase in the online store.

You can contact See Sport Run™ via postal service at:

See Sport Run
191 University Blvd., #503
Denver, CO 80206
1-877-SEE S RUN

JEOPARDY!™ is the trademark of
Sony Pictures Entertainment.

Major League Baseball, MLB, National League, American League,
and World Series are trademarks or service marks
of Major League Baseball Properties, Inc.

USA Pro Edition

© 2003 Sports Education Enterprises, Inc.

<u>Notes</u>

Notes

Notes

Take Me Out to the Ball Game – but Then What?

This **See Sport Run**™ **Spectator's Guide** is for people challenged to understand the great American game of baseball. To know if this is you (or a loved one), take the quick quiz below and check all that apply:

_____ I think a "balk" is one of those waltz moves my grandparents used to do.

_____ I think a "squeeze play" is an off-off-Broadway show about Mr. Whipple's fascination with Charmin.

_____ I think watching baseball is neck 'n neck with watching paint dry.

_____ I think going to a baseball game is a great time to catch up on the latest gossip.

_____ When someone yells "bunt," I think of those fattening doughnut-shaped cakes with icing dribbled on top.

If you checked one or more of the above, this pocket guide is for you!

Visit us at SeeSportRun.com to learn more about additional sports, order other books, purchase merchandise, or provide comments about this book.